Poems from the Midnight

Davy Edge

To Dear Jean,

Love, Light & Peace

Davy S—
xx

First published in July 2018

© Davy Edge 2018

ISBN:
978-1-78926-299-5

Published by Independent Publishing Network

www.davyedge.wordpress.com

Printed by Relay Print, Wallasey, UK

This book is dedicated to the memory of my Mum and Dad, Dot and Tom, for their unfailing love, patience, and guidance.

PREFACE

Dear Reader,
First and foremost;
thank you for reading these odes.
There's a lot of sweat and blood involved,
and tears, by the bucket load.

My heart and soul is in here, too;
as is my subconscious brain;
as is every memory I have,
for the poet must know of joy and of pain.

So, as you peruse my humble words,
I pray you take something away;
maybe a snippet to make you smile,
or a thought, to brighten your day.

Either way, I'd like to say
"Thank you for buying this book!"
It contains my Life experience;
a whole three years it took!

Please keep me by your bedside;
not in some dusty old case;
and I will be there to dip into,
when you need a moment of grace.

Think of me as a desert isle,
where you can be alone;
we'll maybe share a thought or two;
maybe some seeds will be sown.

But mostly, I hope you're entertained,
away from the daily grind,
as I share with you the fripperies
of my bipolar mind.

I hope it holds some meaning for you,
and that it passes your time;
I also hope you find value
for your £7.99... :) x

FOREWORD

I first met Davy on a November morning in 1982 when he turned up to rehearsals for Blood Brothers with a script under one arm, and a skateboard under the other.
He has more strings to his bow than anyone I've ever known . . . from sword fencing to sailing, stage fighting to surfing, horse riding to dog-whispering. He is a singer, songwriter, guitarist, who also plays piano and cittern . . . the list goes on and on.
The man's a polymath.
And now, this book of poetry has been added to that list.
It is an honour and a pleasure to call him my friend.

Andrew Schofield
July 2018

CONTENTS

Infinite	1
Porridge	2 and 3
An Interesting Guest	4
Dicentra	5
Charity begins at Home	6 and 7
Basket Case	8 and 9
Heart	10
I Would	11
If Music be the Food of Love	12
For Libby (Whoever she may be)	13
Other Eden	14
Sailing	15
A Kidder Conversation	16 and 17
The Beautiful Madness	18 and 19
The Bicycle	20
The Model	21
The Moon and Me	22
The Path	23
A Big Bag of Yesterday	24
A Dog's Life	25
After the Rains	26
Backpack	27
Be	28
Behind the Mask	29
The Train into Town	30 and 31
The Zombie Invasion	32
To My Imaginary Child (on Father's Day)	33
A Terrible Beauty	34
Absent Friends	35
Afterglow	36
Boy	37
Demons in the Undertow	38
Driven	39
In the Event of Fire	40

CONTENTS

Golf	41
Small Thoughts	42
Summer's End	43
Up to the Bus Stop	44
The Forgotten Drawer	45
Kiss	46
In Winter	47
I Would	48
Willow	49
Forget me Not	50
Growth	51
I am Autumn	52
In Praise of Tea	53
A Drinking Song	54
My Pet Hate	55
I Understand	56
Life's Too Short	57
Magenta	58 and 59
Mindgame	60 and 61
On Following the Advice of Poets	62
The Owl	63
Poetry in Emotion	64
Snowfall	65
Pep Talk	66
Sunset Over Clieves Hill	67
Rock n' Roll Dinosaur	68 and 69
The Elbow	70
On Music	71
The Mouse's Tale	72 and 73
The Man in the Street	74 and 75
The Singletons	76
Thoughts at Eventide	77
You Are	78
La Vie de Bohême	79

Infinite

I am infinite . . .
There was no beginning.
I have always been;
the frame I was born into,
bound in perishable skin.
It is the ricketty transport,
which holds the light within.
Trees may grow upon its ash,
and Nature flourish there;
when the gift of the physical,
gone in a flash,
is given relief from care;
and I am free to roam once more,
here and everywhere.
Comes not the spring after winter?
Comes not the fruit on the vine?
Comes not the flower, out of its grave,
time, after time, after time?
And so shall I, as a phoenix rise,
with each and every line.
There is no middle.
All is continuous.
There is no end.
I am infinite . . .

Porridge

Porridge!
Scotland's breakfast dish!
Setter-up for the day!
Walter Scott and Rabbie Burns
were sustained this way.
Even William Wallace,
prior to his death,
would have asked for porridge,
while he still had breath.
It sticketh to the sides,
and more,
and fills the hungry tum.
The whole is greater than the sum of its parts.
It's how Life's race is run.
It's healthier than a fry-up,
and does the insides more good
than greasy meat, and runny eggs,
and puddings of pigs' blood.
Grown in the earth,
and harvested,
packaged, and sold on the shelves;
it is the greatest morning gift
we can give ourselves!
Three minutes with milk in the microwave,
You can make it savoury, or sweet.
Add honey, salt, or golden syrup,
then take your spoon and eat!

It's a quick and easy recipe,
and can be made with relatively no pain.
Once you've fallen for its taste,
you'll have it again, and again!
Porridge, then!
The answer to all!
The dietary heaven!
If asked to rate it out of ten,
I'd have to say eleven!

An Interesting Guest

In the dying hours of Channel Four,
Who came hop-hop-hopping
through my chamber door?
His throat a-throbbing, his skin tawny brown;
as bold as brass he came on down.
The galliard, the a la ronde, he danced
with the bewildered dog.
Then returned he to the pond;
an interesting guest,
the garden frog.

Dicentra

Just a row of bleeding hearts,
hanging on a line.
Each year they come to taunt me,
around about this time.
For they, too, seem so sick of love;
their time is here, then gone;
and yet they show their beauty
to each and everyone.
They dazzle and dance in the afternoon breeze,
and, like love, have their day.
No summer dreams will warm them, though,
for soon, they'll fade away.
They flourish in the springtime,
as Love itself takes wing;
they make their mark in April and May,
when blackbird and robin sing.
All good things must come to pass,
and come June, they'll be gone.
Just another bleeding heart,
is Mother Nature's son.

Charity begins at Home

I'm a terror for Ted Baker shirts,
and Italian tailored suits.
I love the feel of a smooth silk scarf,
and old Doc Marten boots.
I've braces and belts, and 'T' shirts and jeans,
and hats of all shapes and sizes.
I've cleaned out every charity shop
from Dundee to Devizes.
I've never spent more than twenty quid
on any particular item.
I don't take friends the same build as me,
in case I have to fight them.
For bargains are a serious matter,
not to be taken lightly.
It's no good buying the first thing you see,
then finding it fits too tightly.
Rather, be patient! It always pays off,
if not today, then tomorrow.
Don't be deterred if you joy is deferred.
Don't suffer from retail sorrow!
For, somewhere, out there on the rails,
a gem is hiding away!
It's made to measure, for business or pleasure,
with no more than a tenner to pay!
So put aside your prejudice,
about wearing pre-loved clothes.
The alternative is the High Street,
and paying through the nose!

Save yourself a bob or two;
the clothes are always clean.
You can look them about, inside and out;
you don't have to look dowdy and mean.
You can buy a swishy outfit;
designer label stuff!
You know, the sort you see in the shops,
when you haven't got enough.
It makes perfect sense to save on the pence,
in these days of hardship and trial.
Take it from me, a charity spree
has all others beat . . . by a mile!

Basket Case

It was exactly the situation I was trying
to avoid.
I now have an over-stuffed hand basket,
and I'm feeling most annoyed.
I should have taken a trolley,
but I couldn't find a pound;
so I went and got a hand basket,
now I'm dragging it around.
There's five pounds of spuds, and a loaf in there;
and I haven't yet got to the cheese.
I've bypassed the section of the
special selection,
and the basket's now down by my knees.
In with the grapes and the rapeseed oil;
in with the banana and apple.
In with the milk and the yoghurt and brie;
now I'm really starting to grapple.
Only two more aisles to go,
and I feel I'm sinking under.
I don't even think I could fit in
a bag of Golden Wonder.
How I managed with the kitchen roll
is anybody's guess.
I have to admit, it's all gone to bits,
in a brie and banana mess.

So next time I'm out shopping,
and I'm tempted to think small,
I'll make sure I have a pound in my hand,
or I'm buying nothing at all!
For baskets are deceiving;
they fill up in a trice.
Next time, I'll take a trolley,
which will be jolly nice . . .

Heart

I am amazed, my bleeding heart!
Beats you yet, though torn apart?
It is a wonder, when all is done,
how the heart, though broken, still lives on.

I Would

I would stroke her neck,
and share with her the secrets
of my ragamuffin mind.
I would write poetry to her
from the deepest chamber of my soul,
and spread my childish words before her
eager gaze.
I would craft melodies to her beauty,
and proclaim love undying
in the dying light.
I would mouth her name to the four winds,
that they may blow fair,
and strew her way with apple blossom.
I would encourage the gypsy in her,
that she may dance,
and know freedom.

If Music Be the Food of Love

If music be the food of love,
my strings are out of tune.
Strange, discordant sounds they make,
beneath the mixed-up moon,
as they serenade the nightjars,
and decorate the gloom.
If music be the food of love,
my song is worn, and tired.
Its meaning has been dulled by time,
its message of hope, expired.
How then, now, to breathe new Life?
How now, to be inspired?
The long in tooth, and the callow youth,
dance to Eros's tune.
The melody plays in the moment,
though the dance has gone too soon;
leaving a memory in its wake,
beneath the mixed-up moon.

For Libby (Whoever She May Be)

Come back with me to Bohemia;
To the home of the brave and the free!
Come back! Come back, O, Libby, my Love,
to the land of afternoon tea!
We'll dine on bream, and vanilla ice cream,
in faded, yesteryear clothes.
I'll light the candles and the fire.
Yes, I'll do both of those!
And you, my Love, shall gather flowers,
and vegetables, in season.
We'll lose ourselves amongst the hours,
and fly in the face of reason!
For reason holds the ties that bind,
and keeps the spirit tame!
Come back with me, O, Libby, my Love,
that our dreams may not be lame!

Other Eden

O, my soul! I am disquieted!
All my visions are
as running water.
Stay! You injurious dream!
Stay awhile!
Let me sink
deep into that mirage
of happy hearts and hopes,
where laughter is commonplace,
and a welcoming awaits my weary tread,
with soothing words, and a pillow for my head.
Let me, one moment longer,
hold on to that other Eden;
that garden of delight,
where I live by day,
and sleep by night.
Let me drink long from that rosy glass,
until this moment comes to pass,
and I am returned again
to my paper, and my pen.

Sailing

I wish I could be with the wind on my neck,
plowing through the foam;
tasting freedom on the for'ard deck,
as the timbers 'round me groan.
I'm filled with Masefield's desire
to go down to the sea again,
and play upon the lyre,
songs for seafaring men.
For they know what it's like to feel alive,
where adventure is commonplace;
barrelling away in a four to five,
the salt spraying up in the face.
Not for them the comforts of home,
the slippers and the fire;
rather they be chilled to the bone,
and raise their voices higher!
On the tide, I'll sail away,
my colours hauled up high;
toward the boundless ocean,
beneath the endless sky.

A Kidder Conversation

Who's the keeper of the flame?
Who's got the light there, laaaa?
I've got a bit of a butt end here,
but it won't go very far.
You're welcome, of course, to have a drag.
You're welcome to have a blow.
"Arhh, eh, la, go easy on that bifter;
I've got me pride, y'know.
Don't go givin' me the soggy end;
I don't want that near me lips.
You robbed it off your Vinnie,
an' he pulls off the tips".
Alright, alright der, cryin' arse,
e'yar, it's your turn now,
Don't say I never give you nothin'.
Eh, what's with the sweaty brow?
"It's made me feel a little bit sickkk.
The end's wet! It's fallin' apart!"
Oh gerrit down yer pipe, and stop
behavin' like a tart.
"E'yar, the thing has gone right out",
Give us yer lighter, lid.
"Alright, alright, I've got the light.
I robbed it off our kid".

And so the conversation goes...
I listen, in disbelief.
Are these the new born Scousers,
with spanners in place of teeth?
It's like a foreign language,
in a foreign land.
"Is right, is right, is right der, la".
I don't know, 'cos I don't understand!
Take me back once more, I beg,
I'm twentieth century Scouse!
I'm left behind in these changing times
by people who've got no nouse!
They've lost the accent exceedingly rare,
and replaced it with a strange little voice.
I'm afraid I'm old school Liverpool.
And that, I remain, by choice!

The Beautiful Madness

She sat and cried for the beautiful madness
of her youth;
for days of fairgrounds and rowing boats,
and innocence;
for days when it was so warm,
no-one wore coats,
not even policemen.
But that was then.
That was when . . . oh, that was when!
Oh, to have those times again,
before the winds blew too cold;
before the days of growing old;
hair, now silver, turned from gold.
She sipped from the chalice of memory,
sepia tinted and ripped apart,
leaving ragged edges,
hanging from her heart;
the heart which gave her strength to dance,
and the foolishness of first romance;
the handsome suitor, the game of chance...
The Game of Chance!
Oh, isn't that Life?
She would have remained a wife,
had not she suffered mental strife,
which led to a changing in her ways,
when the husband,
in search of better days,
left her as the leaves were turning brown.
Now it is winter, and her snow hair has
grown thin.

She keeps loose change in a biscuit tin,
to give to the poor,
should they knock on her door.
But nobody knocks there anymore.
Yet, the thing she misses most, in truth,
is the beautiful madness of her youth.

The Bicycle

The bicycle stood where he had left it,
chained to a tree.
He went to war from there,
and never came home; (lost at sea).
Its rust encrusted frame,
testament to the years,
still bore the logo 'Triumph',
the irony obscured by the marauding ivy;
the ground around it, stained with tears.
The cracked, black leather seat, faded under the sun of seventy summers,
its oils rain-washed away, was now home to wildlife.
On the weather-worn basket,
spiders wove their webs of the day.
He had no wife,
but his mother had placed fresh flowers,
each week until her death.
She had spent quiet hours
with his name on her breath,
and had been no stranger to wars,
losing her husband to a previous cause.
(At Ypres, a machine gun had ripped through his vest
as he tried to take a machine gun nest).
Although the bell no longer rings,
it calls to politicians.
How many bicycles will be left to rot,
before there's an end to munitions?

The Model

Majestic, her deportment;
as smooth as silk, her skin;
he fingers through the assortment
of pencils in his tin.
Her outline falls on paper;
each curve and feature, etched;
her secrets, harboured safe inside;
his imagination, stretched.
He makes an attempt to catch her eye;
she stares off into space;
and all of his shortcomings
are naked in their disgrace.
As a statuette of marble,
motionless, she stands.
He dreams to catch her universe
in his foolish, mortal hands.
Her face always eludes him,
It keeps him from the whole;
for there is no artist's tool
which knows
the essence of her soul...

The Moon and Me

Damn the dreams which keep me from sleep.
The wide awake hours bring reverie deep.
Damn the thoughts which crowd my head,
when all the world's asleep in bed.
In the half-light, half alive,
cast adrift and left to survive;
is it only me on the angry sea?
Have the others managed to struggle free?
The lighthouse flickers,
and then goes out.
No answer, then.
No friendly shout.
And I am alone, just the moon and me;
it was ever thus, and shall ever be.

The Path

There are no signposts along my route.
No previous footfall,
by which to measure my step.
The ground is clear,
up to my last hack.
I am off the beaten track;
and though the sky be black,
I press forward,
into the unknown.
I have shown no great courage,
nor made heroic gesture.
Curiosity is my handmaiden,
and forever she tends my needs,
as I make my way, ever onward,
among the flowers, and the weeds.

A Big Bag of Yesterday

The last thing I put down last night
was a big bag of yesterday.
It was hard to sleep with it on my back,
so, on the floor it had to stay.
As much as I tried to close my eyes,
my attention was drawn away,
to that heavy heap beside the bed;
that big bag of yesterday.
I emptied it onto the mat.
My angry words fell out,
as did thoughts that I shouldn't have had,
as did fear, and doubt.
I tried to put them all back in,
to deal with on the morrow;
it was then I realised,
the bag contained much sorrow.
Better to leave it open,
and let it drain away,
than face it again tomorrow,
that big bag of yesterday.
Today, I stepped with confidence,
light of shoulder and mind.
I waved to the big bag of yesterday,
as I left it far behind!

A Dog's Life

Quietly, the morning began...
drizzling rain;
a dog and his man.
A dog and his man!
What a glorious pair!
Epitome of devotion!
Example of care!
Only Love behind those eyes;
no hidden agendas,
no hurtful disguise.
Faithful Retainer!
His master's own!
In soul, and heart,
adoration alone.
Loyal to the hand that feeds,
who caters for his daily needs,
the honest dog has no sides at all,
his only desire, the throw of a ball.
A dog and his man;
what a glorious pair!
Many lessons can be learned from there.

After the Rains

After the rains,
we sat on the wet swings,
and kicked our feet;
the damp on the seats
soaking through our jeans.
"I know what this means" you said,
as the fading rainbow behind your head
returned to its mystery.
You claimed that we were different people,
and that the rains had affected everybody.
Nothing would be the same for anybody,
anymore.
The rains had brought about new thinking.
The old ways had trickled out of style,
down a dirty gully, and into the drains.
Nothing could be the same, after the rains.
We could now go out without our coats on,
to enjoy the freshness of the air.
Everywhere, there were people.
People who had changed, apparently;
yet everyone still looked the same.
You said "transformation begins in the brain."
Everyone did look more knowing,
I must admit.
But I hadn't changed; not one little bit.

Backpack

Life requires a backpack;
filled with the necessary tools;
glue, to mend a broken heart;
a hammer, to break the rules;
a spirit level, for obvious reasons;
a sextant, to steer by the stars;
a saw, to cut away the past,
and remove the iron bars.
For, sometimes, we're imprisoned
in cages we've designed.
We need a good old jemmy bar,
to open up the mind!
Also, have a pencil
to jot down new ideas;
and don't forget a rubber,
to erase your worries and fears.
It pays to carry a compass,
so that your feet may tread
only, ever, always,
on your path ahead.
Finally, a match you'll need,
to set your soul alight;
to shine out in the darkness,
and brighten up the night.
For Life's a hard and rocky road,
where the lesson comes after the test.
If we have a trusty backpack,
we can be considered blessed!

Be

Be.
Stop doing.
Take a moment.
Be.
Just Be.

Behind the Mask

Is it you who's hiding behind the mask?
You look so concealed, I'm afraid to ask!
You never give a thing away,
and so we go on with the play:
"Weather's awful. The 'flu bug is rife."
(We neatly avoid the subject of Life).
That would mean you opening up;
and you'd rather smash your favourite cup,
than let me see you as you are,
exposing every single scar.
But, when those scars are out on view,
that's when you're being the real you.
For beauty is found only in truth;
that much holds, for adult and youth.
If the mask should ever slip,
and the honest truth falls from your lip,
I'm sure it would a picture paint
of who you are, without constraint!

The Train into Town

The train was full of commuters,
on the journey into town.
I was fortunate to be on the thing,
let alone be sitting down.
People were stood up like sardines,
in a giant, moving tin;
hanging on the straps above;
silent, in their skin.
The woman across the way from me
was reading a book on marriage.
Another tried to calm her child,
further on up the carriage.
I was struggling with seventeen across . . .
'Deviant Croatian'.
I could feel him breathing down my neck,
as we pulled into a station.
"I think you'll find that's 'raincoat'"
He said with smug little grin.
One day, I thought, he'll pick the wrong sort,
and someone will do him in.
The ticket inspector had started her rounds;
I took mine from my pocket.
A gang of youths had told untruths,
and shot off like a rocket.
A motley crew of passengers
we were, on the eight-fifteen;
all bundled together for half an hour,
It was like some horrible dream.

It gave me joy to take the air,
when I had climbed above ground.
I won't be in such a hurry, next time,
to take the train into town.

The Zombie Invasion

I fear not the zombie invasion.
It's here, right now, in every nation.
People walking around in droves,
staring at phones, stuck under the nose.
You never get a 'Good day' from them,
those text-obsessed women,
and you tube-mad men.
It's pointless trying to converse;
you end up being ignored, and what's worse
they're not even listening;
you're wasting your breath,
you go away yet nearer death,
without a word being passed between
you and the person with their head
in the screen.
It's a killer of conversation,
which I regard an abomination.
People are losing the art of speech,
as long their phone's within easy reach.
It really is a maddening bore
watching someone play with their iPhone 4.
Put the damn thing down! How rude!
I am with your nerve imbued!
I'm not, by nature, a violent man,
so let me warn you while I can;
if anyone plays with their phone in future,
they'll be going home in need of a suture.

To My Imaginary Child
(on Father's Day)

I'm sorry I was never here
for your presence to appear.
My heart was always on the wing;
so we lost out, poor Dear!
I'd have really enjoyed your childhood;
I'm sure I'd have spoiled you rotten.
I'd have bought your clothes in John Lewis's,
with your undies made of cotton.
We'd have shared the bond which comes along
between a parent and child,
had I not been so foolish;
had I not been so wild.
I'd have striven to educate your mind,
to practice independent thought.
For there are important things to learn,
which, from a book, can't be taught.
I hope that you would have manners,
and always say 'thank you' and 'please';
be generous in your nature,
and give of yourself with ease.
I hope that you would be a Light,
for, around, the world is dark.
and that you'd embrace your passion,
and not worry about making your mark.
All of these things, I'd have wished for you,
but it wasn't in the stars,
so I spent your university money
on several nice guitars.

A Terrible Beauty

I was an adventurer,
and a lover.
My heart was aflame with passion and Life.
I did not feel the sun
searing my wings
until it was too late.
Crash and burn!
Crash and burn!
Done to a crisp at every turn!
Now, the poet rises up,
from the flickering embers;
not phoenix-like, at all;
rather awkwardly, in fact,
struggling to the feet like a new-born foal,
yet cold of heart and sick of soul.

Absent Friends

I still go about my day.
The logs are burning on the fire,
but, in some wistful way,
I, to my chair, retire.
There are empty places around the room,
where once sat friends of mine.
Memories of honoured ghosts,
who transcend the trappings of time.
For they have left their love here;
in each song they remain.
Their presence is in every verse,
and every sweet refrain.
And so, by eternity, we are bound.
May each be blessed to know;
it is a joy to leave some love
behind us, when we go.
It soothes awhile the grieving heart,
and comforts the aching soul;.
until we reach that better place,
where the broken are made whole.

Afterglow

I compose you like a song,
and bring out your hidden nuances
To capture you in melody is my Life's work;
for you are the tune which occupies my daydreams,
and haunts my sleeping hours.
Light and shade.
Light and shade.
Both, good use of
must be made.
For you are not as hot and cold;
but as fire and ice.
The world is your lover,
and your enemy.
It contains for you the highest heaven,
and the basest hell.
Ebb and Flow;
to and fro;
calm, now, in the afterglow.
When the tide has gone to sleep,
demons doze and angels weep.

Boy

If I were to talk to you now, boy,
what would I have to say?
What would be our subject,
if we conversed today?
Maybe I would sit you down,
and tell you what I know.
The fool speaks in his ignorance,
to the child from long ago.
Perchance you could enlighten me
on keeping you alive;
for if I lose your spirit, boy,
t'would mean I would merely survive.
And what good is paltry survival,
to the adventurous mind?
What use fear, and loneliness,
sent to torment the blind?
To look at Life through child-like eyes,
Is, surely, our greatest boon.
The adult overthinks too much
to sing an innocent tune.
Let me chant your melody,
and keep you in my soul;
We'll walk the road together, boy;
for the part is now made whole.

Demons in the Undertow

We all have demons.
Some disguise themselves as skeletons,
and hide in the wardrobe,
among the happy clothes,
in a hat you once wore,
to look like Zsa Zsa Gabor,
showing off the coat of Plenty.
Bone deep! Bone deep!
O! The secrets that we keep!
We fear our sudden nakedness,
exposed for the world to see;
leaving ourselves empty.
Vacuous void! Vacuous void!
Everything is now destroyed!
All the truths are out on show,
The demons reach up from below,
and I am pulled away

Driven

If I awake in the morning,
and I am still here,
I'll face the day with fortitude;
not excuses; not fear.
I'll aim to make things happen;
I won't sit, and wait around.
My journey calls me onward,
where opportunities abound!
For if I do not seize the day,
I waste the time which is given.
I've exchanged a day of my Life for today,
so let me, by my purpose, be driven!
Let me touch a lonely heart,
or hold an aching soul.
Let my words find brokenness,
and recreate the whole.
Give to me the wiser mind,
and a listening ear;
some comfort may another find,
in a moment of cheer.
If I awake in the morning,
and I am still here.

In the Event of Fire

In the event of fire,
burning in the soul,
do not call the fire brigade;
but put on some more coal.
Fan the flames with all of your might,
and let your passions roar;
and if the fire should dwindle at all,
add more fuel, as before.
Let it rage, at any cost,
and light up the world around.
For too many souls live in darkness,
too many, by half, I've found.
Each of us has a little spark,
but some never let it ignite;
They gorge on negativity,
and live their lives in fright.
Therefore, be you not afraid
of the holiness of fire.
It comes to feed the spirit,
that burning of desire.
It comes to ease the heavy heart;
it comes to lift us higher.
Therefore, do not panic,
in the event of fire.

Golf

I've never got the game of golf.
I stand beside Mark Twain.
It's a good walk wasted,
to my unappreciative brain.
Standing on the fairway,
slicing at the ball,
must be someone's cup of tea,
but it's not mine, at all.
I'd rather balance on a wave,
in the early morning sun;
or race a horse along a beach,
than claim a hole-in-one.
I find the whole thing too sedate,
not death defying enough.
I'd rather have my balls in my mouth,
than lose them in the rough.
Forgive my obvious ignorance,
But I barely see the point
of thwacking a ball around a field,
and knocking myself out of joint.
Each to their own, quite rightly so.
That's ethically sound.
Understand, if I don't join you,
next time you play a round.

Small Thoughts

It would be good to think small thoughts;
to concern myself with the garden around me,
instead of creating vast landscapes
of gargantuan proportions.
Let me study one single flower;
its petals, and its stem,
rather than follow the overwhelming urge
to play among a field of daffodils,
and give myself to their dancing.
For my legs tire,
and my mind is dizzy from adventure.
Settle, now.
Settle, now,
in the blue gold of the forget-me-not.

Summer's End

When the last over of summer has been bowled,
and a chill hangs on the evening air,
we throw on our jumpers to keep out the cold,
and greet September with mild despair.
Goodbye to sizzling barbeque days,
and garden conversations;
planning camping holidays,
and structural alterations.
Goodbye to strawberries and cream on the lawn;
goodbye to morning haze;
hello to Autumn in customary brown,
farewell to longer days.
And so the seasons turn again,
and Nature calls her tune.
A gentle rain begins to fall,
beneath a harvest moon.

Up to the Bus Stop

Up to the bus stop,
onto the bus.
What is to become of us?
Into work for quarter to nine;
stamp your card,
man the line.
Toil the day through,
half-alive;
put on your coat
at quarter to five.
Home for dinner,
meat and two veg.
Tomorrow is turkey;
you live on the edge.
Soaps on tv, stroke the cat,
put the bin out.
After that?
Climb the stairs,
it's time for bed.
Don't worry about dying,
you're already dead.

The Forgotten Drawer

Will somebody tell me what I need this
thing for,
and why it still lives in the
forgotten drawer;
full of instructions for now defunct phones,
pieces of string and old incense cones . . .
Manuals for this, and manuals for that.
A photo of someone in a blue and white hat . . .
Nails I was keeping, just in case . . .
Bluetacked together, to save some space . . .
A rusty old compass, in case I get lost,
now stuck to the Bluetack,
its maker embossed . . .
A watch that stopped sometime at
a quarter past three . . .
A leaflet that boasts
'Get Your Loft Lagged For Free' . . .
A small piece of wood that jammed open
a door . . .
Will somebody tell me what I need this
thing for?

Kiss

I dreamed
that somewhere between the
midnight and the morning,
there was you;
that all the world's strange madness,
took on a different hue.
I fancied that the sadness in such a
world as this,
could suddenly be lifted,
in the moment of a kiss.

In Winter

In winter, we tend to hide away,
hibernate 'til a warmer day;
sit by fires, drink mulled wine,
to celebrate the Christmastime.
Opening presents, festive fun.
Christmas Day is second to none.
Switch on the lights around the tree;
all about, a happiness spree!
But, think of those living on their own,
as you chomp your turkey down to the bone.
To some, it's just another day,
spent alone, in the same old way.
No special meal, no cracker to pull;
all in all, it's incredibly dull.
They spend the day in a silent state;
a radio keeps them up to date,
playing carols from gatherings of choirs,
from inside the world of steeples and spires.
No human contact is, sadly, their lot,
being the ones the others forgot.
When the spirit of the day is to share,
a thought for them, this Christmas, spare.

I Would

I would stroke her neck,
and share with her the secrets
of my ragamuffin mind.
I would write poetry to her
from the deepest chamber of my soul,
and spread my childish words before
her eager gaze.
I would craft melodies to her beauty,
and proclaim love undying
in the dying light.
I would mouth her name to the four winds,
that they may blow fair,
and strew her way with apple blossom.
I would encourage the gypsy in her,
that she may dance,
and know freedom.

Willow

Willow, weep,
and hang your head.
Accompany me as I mourn my dead.
Tears can never fall in vain;
from tree or man, 'tis all the same.
Loss is never an easy bear,
this world being full of weighty care.
Yet they have slipped the shackles of earth,
that base planet which gave them birth;
and in my heart they sing again,
those braves, those diamonds,
those merry men!
Willow, weep, for we shall never
see their like again.

Forget me Not

Forget me not, when I am gone.
Let something of me still live on.
For in the wildflower, I am reflected,
and grow free, though rejected.
In your garden, once I bloomed,
alongside roses, tall, and pruned.
In abundance, I flourished;
in want, I died.
"Forget me not!" the lover cried.

Growth

Everybody suffers
in one way, or another;
our demons are our own.
Growth is painful, in times of grief,
or when we grow alone.
But grow, we must,
through stones, and dust,
if we are to understand;
naught may be built on rue and regret,
no more than on quicklime, or sand.
Everybody suffers,
in one way, or another;
by each, let this be heard.
Pain and pleasure are equal in measure,
no human Life is spared.
And yet the sun
still shines for some,
who look for rainbows through rain.
Life is but a learning curve,
in a vast, eternal game.
For souls we are,
and beings we be.
Mortality is our fate.
Let us take this time to Live!
Before it's all too late!

I am Autumn

I have Lived!
O! How I have Lived!
I have felt the rush of salt water to my tail,
and ridden the rolling wave!
I have shared the wind with an Arabian
horse at full gallop,
along a beach of endless sand,
and sailed the sea on catamaran;
just the breeze, the sun, and me.
Now, I am Autumn,
and slower of gait,
(breathing more heavily, of late).
The fiery reds and brilliant yellows,
which so characterised my salad days
have mellowed into pastel shades.
Shoes wear out, and glitter fades.
But I have lived.
O! How I have lived.
The changing leaves display the remnants
Of such a colourful spring and summer,
Lived out, to wild degree!
But, now, I am Autumn,
and those memories
are my history.

In Praise of Tea

By the power invested in me,
I'd like to praise the cup of tea!
Not that coffee doesn't have its place;
it can sober you up, and save you disgrace.
Though, on a morning's early rise,
there is but one sight for sore eyes.
The caddy, in its glory, stands,
containing leaves from foreign lands.
Ah, to breathe their heady scent;
the aroma of the Orient!
Soon, the tea is in the cup;
the day is suddenly looking up.
Sugared, or not, boiling hot,
brewed up in a china pot,
the working man has lived by its code,
as I have, in my own abode.
And, of an evening, settled down,
if the day has been a thorny crown,
and Life has thrown lemons, let it be;
treat yourself to a biscuit, maybe.
Let the world go drifting by,
kick off your shoes and loosen your tie,
Take a moment to be free.
It's amazing, the power of a cup of tea!

A Drinking Song

My lonely, lost, and loveless friend,
I've been where you are now.
I've walked that dreary one-way street,
wondering why, and how.
I almost drowned in self-pity,
and wished that the end had been near;
rather than face tomorrow,
next week, next month, next year.
And so, I drank another drink,
and hoped it would go away;
that burgeoning feeling of helplessness,
which met me every day.
The more you drink, the more you think.
The circle never ends;
it only increases in density,
and all reality, bends.
I've sat, head bowed, as you do now,
and stared, long, at the floor;
ignoring the ring of the telephone,
and the knocking on the door.
I've banged my head against the wall,
in sheer frustration and rage;
I've sought so hard to end the pain,
I'm surprised I've reached this age.
My friend, I've sat where you are now.
One day, you'll sit with me,
conscious of the good things,
which come with sobriety.

My Pet Hate

Nothing to the right of them!
Nothing to the left of them!
Still they insist to remain,
sat at sixty miles per hour,
those hoggers of the middle lane!
They've obviously paid their road tax,
and think they have a choice!
TWO AND THREE ARE OVERTAKING LANES!
I apologise for raising my voice...
I have to ask what it is with you
that you need to be in the middle?
It's something I don't understand,
an enigmatic riddle...
You're clogging up the motorway,
with your need to take up space;
and every car behind you
holds an angry driver's face.
It is extremely poor driving,
forcing souls to undertake
dangerous manoeuvres,
foot, hovering on the brake.
Get into the inside lane,
if you're trundling along;
and check up on your Highway Code,
'cause what you're doing is wrong!

I Understand

I lived my life in half-light,
confounded by the drink.
It takes away all reason,
and clarity to think.
It took away my sense of worth,
and victimised my mind;
'til nothing remained but constant doubt;
all confidence, left behind.
It strips away motivation,
and kills the creative muse.
There's nothing in the memory bank;
nothing at all you can use.
Everything halts at self-pity;
that all-consuming Hell.
Self-respect and harmony
are sold down the river, as well.
I pray these words may touch an ear,
and be a helping hand.
Freedom is only a whisper away.
I know.
I understand.

Life's Too Short

Life's too short to wear polyester,
or use inferior margarine
that's a molecule away from plastic.
Make butter a choice, not a dream.
Get rid of the rusty razor blade,
that rips your face away.
Treat yourself to a new one,
for it's how you start your day.
Be kind to yourself, and expect the best.
Wear your favourite hat.
To hell with what the others think.
Life's too short for all that.
Be as you as you can be,
there's no time like the now.
Don't reach the end of your allotted span,
wondering why, and how.
Seek your higher purpose;
Pick up your dreams from the mat.
Don't spend your days in self-pity;
Life's too short for all that.
Don't waste your time complaining.
Don't let your bubble go flat;
and get rid of the polyester;
Life's too short for all that.

Magenta

She said her name was Magenta;
her hair was flaming red.
She ignored the signals I sent her,
so I leaned toward discourse instead.
She told me she was Capricorn,
and that her mother was Greek.
I couldn't help but notice
the softness of her cheek.
The daylight hours in which she lived,
were blessed by the sound of her voice,
which lilted freely on the air;
freedom being her choice.
She had that cool, Bohemian look;
her eyes, as green as grass.
I found myself intoxicated,
and hoped the moment would pass.
For she was a visitor to this world;
the Universe was her home.
She said she liked to travel,
and that she travelled alone.
Her lips, as red as poinsettia,
broke into a smile.
She laughed the laugh of children
who remain forever wild.
I'll never forget Magenta,
with the hair of flaming red;
for she wasn't quite like anybody else,
who dream their dreams in bed.

She lived a life of adventure,
with great, swashbuckling style;
that rarity of nature,
the girl with the poinsettia smile.

Mindgame

I write until my brain aches,
and ink stains the paper
with my untidy thoughts.
O! That there were some shape to them,
those fleeting shadows!
Scanty in their attire, they fall over each other
in their awkward gracelessness,
and strew the floor with muttered obscenities.
I am no stranger to their darkness,
those denizens of the night!
They sap my soul of purpose,
and put my joy to flight!
Still, I court their attention;
for they are better than nothing at all.
Nothing begets nothing!
Words! Screwed up in a ball!
O! That I could tame those thoughts
to act upon my whim!
To be the master of my mind,
to rid my soul of sin!
Yet, Journeyman to grief am I.
No refuge here to find.
To hell with thoughts I can't control,
and all of their hellish kind!
Bring me flowers to bedeck my hall,
that I may take their scent;
that they may breathe atonement,
and bring forth merriment.
Give to me my heart's desire,
and all else I forego!

Send to me the inner fire,
to melt away the snow!
I write until my brain aches,
and my demons laugh from below.

On Following the Advice of Poets

Robert Frost! Robert Frost!
On the road not taken,
I think I'm lost!
I did as you, and beat my path;
now I'm as tormented as Sylvia Plath.
I shouldn't have given the heart, Willie Yeats;
sound advice, but alas, too late!
I am, I am, as John Clare knows,
the self-consumer of my woes!
George Gordon Byron! My thinking's not right.
Shall I go no more a-roving,
so late into the night?
Such wisdom from these great minds fall,
Which should I follow? None, or all?
As each presents a different illusion,
needs must, I come to my own conclusion.
Life can be measured as a garden flower.
We seed, we blossom, then, gone is our hour.
If in that time our purpose we find,
we achieve Nirvana – peace of mind!
For surely this must be our goal;
to have that peace in mind and soul.
What other gain is our employ,
if not to fill the world with joy?
So, Mr Shakespeare, I'll listen to you,
for to thine own self, one must be true.
And to other poets who offer advice
on Life, and Love, and dealing with mice,
I have, to conclude, but this to say:
I'm better going my own sweet way!

The Owl

Silence.
Then,
the owl.
Wit-to-woo...
Wit-to-woo...
under the cowl of night.
Then,
silence.
The light from a single candle
keeps me company,
as I sit down to write.
Nothing.
Then,
the words begin
to
come,
one
at
a
time.
Then,
a flurry of phrases
spring to mind.
Some of them neatly
for rhyme designed.
Silence.
Then,
the owl.
Wit-to-woo...
Wit-to-woo...
O! That I had his wit to woo!

Poetry in Emotion

I would my heart were made of steel;
then, I would not need to feel.
Too oft, in reverie, I have idled;
succumbed to passion, yet unbridled;
forsook good reason with hasty action;
courted not dissatisfaction.
And yet, in pieces, I am bound;
all of them, brittle love unfound!
Must the poet's song be so,
in order that deep words may flow?
For happiness engenders gain;
who, then would pray for floods of rain,
to fill the page with sad refrain?
For sadness solely engenders pain.
I would my heart were made of steel,
and Life, soft-focus, more unreal.
Alas, it is the poet's way
to absorb emotions, night, and day;
to suffer consequence of thought,
accepting all, rejecting nought,
'til paper screams with scratch of pen;
beauty from sorrow created again.

Snowfall

There's something romantic about snowfall,
when it's delightfully new.
It's met with mixed emotion,
yet, loved by the innocent few.
For innocence comes dressed in white;
unsullied, and unknown.
And then it soon is swept away,
when the wind has blown.
There's something romantic about snowfall,
in a picture-postcard way.
It leads us to a wonderland,
where dreams don't go astray.
It leads to thoughts of childishness,
and breaking of one's chains;
and making the most of playtime,
before the coming of the rains.
There's something romantic about snowfall.
Its day is here, and then gone.
It stays awhile in beauty,
and then, its work is done.
And so, we, like the snowfall,
must come and go, in time.
Better, then, to sparkle,
and Live the Life sublime!

Pep Talk

I sat and talked with Worry,
for half an hour or more.
He really had me going,
until I showed him the door.
Next up came No Confidence,
who made me want to die!
I was almost in submission,
when Acceptance caught my eye.
"Whatever is to be, will be"
he whispered in my ear.
"All this worry won't change a thing;
neither will living in fear."
"Live for today, not tomorrow.
As for yesterday, it's in the past.
Nothing we do can change that now,
so stop going nowhere fast!
Hold yourself in the moment,
be true to yourself in your way,
be everything you've dreamed of,
this second, this minute, this day!
For time, in haste, is marching on,
and quickly comes the hour;
so make the most of all you have;
free up your inner power.
Promise yourself you'll never again
be stressed, near half to death.
Relax your shoulders, and your arms,
be aware of your measured breath.
Take time in the day to 'be';
slow your hurried pace;
and may you feel the benefits
of wondrous Nature's grace!"

Sunset Over Clieves Hill

Sunset;
and grey, bubbled clouds
rise from Welsh hills,
like fluffy mountains,
curling upward
through reddened sky.
The lights of Liverpool
twinkle in the distance,
like ghosts of forgotten stars.
The evening is still.
No breeze;
the trees,
magnificently motionless,
keep watch over the stretching fields.

Rock n' Roll Dinosaur

Brut! Denim! Soap on a Rope!
These were the things which gave us hope.
Hai Karate! Paco Rabanne!
We knew how to Live it, man.
Saturday flicks, and teenage kicks;
going to my cousin's on the forty-six;
Weekend work in a fashion boutique,
make a few quid to get me through the week.
I'm a child of the seventies, fearless and bold;
the twenty-first century leaves me cold.
I wouldn't like to be young again
in tomorrow's world. It'd be a sin.
I'm a rock 'n' roll dinosaur,
out in the cold, too cold to thaw.
Frozen, in a moment in time,
when I got the girl and made her mine.
Sad to say, she went on her way,
and I, my emotions on display,
cried and cried all the way home.
How would I walk through the world alone?
But chicken in a basket cured the down;
that, and a few cans of Newcastle Brown.
Every generation thinks theirs is the best,
But, I tell you now, we were totally blessed.
The finest music from a golden age,
when tie-dye and flares were all the rage.

Now, I feel like a grumpy old man,
watching all around me go down the pan.
I'll stop, and I'll go on no more.
Yours,
The Rock 'n' Roll Dinosaur.

The Elbow

I think I loved her
more than she liked me.
She told me it was over,
as she poured a cup of tea,
and dripped essential oils
on a bowl of pot pourri.
I thought it was important
to share her deepest thought.
She seemed to be more bothered
about the shoes she'd bought,
while I, in silence, hovered;
(we never, ever, fought).
It presented an awkward moment,
her mother's untimely call;
she didn't flinch,
not even an inch,
as she hoovered down the hall,
picking up the remains of my dreams
'til there was nothing at all.
I think I loved her
more than she liked me.
I came to that conclusion,
as I handed back her key,
and made my way out for the very last time;
a page in her history.

On Music

Music is a beauteous muse,
for keeping demons low.
She fills a chasm in my heart;
that, no man else can know,
and soothes the silent aching,
which follows wher'er I go.

She is the constant lover,
in whom I take delight;
and every sacred moment shared,
bathes me in her light,
and stops my mind from wandering,
through corridors of night.

Frailty is not her name,
nor fickleness her trait.
Faithful is her nature,
and Loyal is her gait.
She never once has broken my heart,
or turned the hand of fate.

The Mouse's Tale

Deep in the heart of the garden,
there lived a tiny mouse.
He rarely showed his little face,
and never came into the house.
He obviously had a family,
for whom he sought to provide;
they lived on seeds and insects,
and anything else he could find.
Then, one day, tragedy befell,
as I spotted next door's cat;
appearing very pleased with himself,
and looking rather fat.
I prayed that the mouse had made good
his escape;
that he'd somehow got back to his nest.
But the dastardly cat had been lying in wait,
with a devilish heart in his breast.
O! Bob! O! Bob! (for so the mouse was named)
What has become of you?
I fear I shall never see you more,
drinking the morning dew.
How cruel is Mother Nature,
in her creation of the cat.
Doesn't she know it's not very nice
to orphan mice like that.
There's silence now in the garden.
The cat's sat on the wall;
I'm ready with my water gun,
should it come down at all.

I'm standing like Clint Eastwood,
and here, I'm going to stay.
I've got my eye trained on you now.
Come on, cat . . . make my day . . .

The Man in the Street

The man in the street,
with the dog at his feet,
and the paper cup in his hand,
is blankly staring forward.
This isn't what he had planned.
A troubled youth, now longer of tooth;
his beard, unkempt, and dirty;
his acquaintances mutter
"he's a bit of a nutter,
who'll probably be dead by thirty."
As if by strange divinity,
I felt a great affinity,
for that man could have been me;
or any of the hundreds of others,
on their weekend shopping spree.
The man in the street,
with the dog at his feet,
looked weary and forlorn.
He told me there are moments
he wishes he'd never been born.
There's a man in the street
with torn shoes on his feet,
in each and every town.
All of them had lives before
misfortune brought them down.
Some are alcoholics;
many are mentally ill.
Receiving no medication,
can be the bitterest pill.

So if you meet the man in the street,
at least pass the time of day.
It could be you, with the hole in your shoe;
and your dog sleeping soundly away.

Singletons

You can always tell the singletons;
they're still awake at night;
long, long, after the lovers,
have curled in their delight.
They have the bathroom to themselves,
and never have to queue.
No need for strange contortions,
whenever they need the loo.
They're used to cooking meals for one,
and go to places, alone.
They talk with friends for hours and hours,
on the telephone.
They always use small trolleys,
and usually pay with cash.
Whenever there's a soul in need,
they have a place to crash.
Where would we be without singletons?
They don't walk around starry-eyed.
They always have a game-plan,
to buffer love denied.

Thoughts at Eventide

What is sweeter, in all this world,
than the brush of a lover's lips?
What, more sensual to know,
than the touch of fingertips,
raking softly down the skin,
nails tracing trails,
purging the soul of the world's dust;
and all that the day entails.
How delightful are unspoken words,
shared in silence;
a conversation of spirits,
and a meeting of minds;
and a oneness,
where two are together entwined.
It is that hope of eternal spring,
which makes the senses dance,
and the heart sing!
And, yet, there is beauty in the night;
and so, I write.
I write.
I write.

You Are

You're Prestat chocolate flakes on a rainy day;
the pealing of bells, on a Sunday in May.
You are the stars in Orion's Belt,
and the spirit of Venus, felt.
You're the scent of flowers growing wild;
the body of a woman, and the heart of a child.
You're a gentle breeze on a warm afternoon;
you bring a smile to the Man in the Moon.
You're all the beauty that is spring;
the song of the lark, when it rises to sing;
You're my favourite song on the radio;
a firefly in the afterglow.
You're an hour of peace in a hundred years' war.
All of these things you are, and more.
It's strange that I should eulogise thus,
when you don't seem to give a tinker's cuss.
So, in my heart, you blaze away,
for you are my prayer, at the end of the day.

La Vie de Bohême

None on earth is richer than I,
for the morning and night are mine.
All things conspire between sun and stars
to create the world sublime.
For I have built up treasures,
beyond material store;
to live the life of the errant king
in the palace of the poor.
My subjects are the destitute,
the broken, and the lost;
and if I have but words to spare,
I give them, without cost.
For words are all my treasury;
I care not for coin or fame.
Such is the poet's lot, my dear.
Such is his spiritual gain.
None on earth is richer than I,
for blessings and wonder are mine.
I yearn not for the kingly crown
of gold and jewels twined.
Enchanted are those moments,
of heart and soul and mind,
as I set sail for Byzantium,
eternal, like Endymion,
in rambling, childish rhyme.